W9-ADL-223

Animal Puzzles

for the Scroll Saw

Second Edition

Date: 10/31/13

745.513 PET
Peterson, Judy
Animal puzzles for the scroll
saw /

PALM BEACH COUNTY
LIBRARY SYSTEM
3650 Summit Boulevard
West Palm Beach, FL 33406-4198

Dedication

This book is dedicated to all of our customers whose suggestions we've adopted and to all of the people who let us take photos of their dogs, horses, cows, etc.

© 2005, 2008 by Fox Chapel Publishing Company, Inc.

Animal Puzzles for the Scroll Saw is an original work, first published in 2005 and revised in 2008 by Fox Chapel Publishing Company, Inc. The patterns contained herein are copyrighted by the authors. Readers may make three copies of these patterns for personal use. The patterns themselves, however, are not to be duplicated for resale or distribution under any circumstances. Any such copying is a violation of copyright law.

ISBN 978–1–56523–391-1

Publisher's Cataloging-in-Publication Data

Peterson, Judy (Judith S.)
    Animal puzzles for the scroll saw / by Judy and Dave Peterson. --
2nd ed. -- East Petersburg, PA : Fox Chapel Publishing, c2008.

    p. ; cm.
    ISBN: 978- 1- 56523- 391- 1
    Includes 20 additional patterns.
    Previous edition: 2005.
    Includes index.

    1. Jigsaw puzzles-- Patterns. 2. Wooden toy making.
3. Woodwork -- Patterns. I. Peterson, Dave (David S.) II. Title.

TT186 .P465 2008
745.51/3--dc22   2008

To learn more about the other great books from Fox Chapel Publishing, or to find a retailer near you, call toll-free 800-457-9112 or visit us at *www.FoxChapelPublishing.com.*

Note to Authors: We are always looking for talented authors to write new books in our area of woodworking, design, and related crafts. Please contact: Acquisition Editor, 1970 Broad Street, East Petersburg, PA 17520.

Printed in Indonesia

First printing
Second printing
Third printing

Because scrolling wood and other materials inherently includes the risk of injury and damage, this book cannot guarantee that creating the projects in this book is safe for everyone. For this reason, this book is sold without warranties or guarantees of any kind, expressed or implied, and the publisher and the authors disclaim any liability for any injuries, losses, or damages caused in any way by the content of this book or the reader's use of the tools needed to complete the projects presented here. The publisher and the authors urge all scrollers to thoroughly review each project and to understand the use of all tools before beginning any project.

Table of Contents

About the Authors

A former schoolteacher and librarian, Judy found her niche in life as a woodworker. She bought her first saw in 1990 and, within the first six months, was cutting and creating her own designs. A winner of many design awards, Judy now sells her puzzles at art and craft shows around the country. Together with her husband, Dave, she has written numerous articles for *Scroll Saw Woodworking & Crafts*, and she teaches scroll sawing at the Woodcraft store in her hometown of Madison, Wisconsin. In her spare time, Judy reads, keeps track of politics on TV, gardens, cooks, turns bowls on her lathe, and puts together other people's flat puzzles.

Dave is officially retired after a career in programming and systems analysis. His interest in and experience with computers, databases, and spreadsheets make him suited to run the record-keeping side of Judy's small business.

In his spare time, Dave reads, is active in the local Macintosh Users' Group, writes the occasional article for the Wisconsin Alliance of Artists and Craftspeople newsletter, and tries to keep up with his wife.

As far as their books and magazine articles go, Judy does all the designing, scrollwork, sanding, and finishing. She also writes all the technical portions. Dave organizes the material, provides a first-draft version for Judy's review, takes the in-process photos, does all of the typing, and interfaces with their editor. All in all, the distribution of duties capitalizes on both their strengths and provides an amicable distribution of labor.

Judy and Dave co-authored an article in the Summer 2005 issue of *Scroll Saw Workshop* magazine, titled "How to Select the Shows and Design your Booth for Maximum Sales."

This book is the result of their third collaboration. Fox Chapel Publishing published their first book, *Dinosaur Puzzles for the Scroll Saw*, in August 2002 and their second book, *Fantasy & Legend Puzzles for the Scroll Saw*, in February 2005.

Introduction

Why interlocking and freestanding puzzles?

I like puzzles. These days, when I'm not making my own puzzles, I'm likely to be doing someone else's. I didn't, however, plan to go into business designing and making jigsaw puzzles. I bought a scroll saw because I have always liked wood and because I was fascinated by the scroll saw work I saw at an art show. In 1989, when my family and I made our annual trek to a nearby Renaissance Fair, I bought a five-piece puzzle as a souvenir. While it was attractive, it was not interlocking, so you really couldn't pick it up without having it fall apart.

When I began designing my own puzzles, I decided all of them would be interlocking so that they could be handled. The puzzles in this book reflect that decision I made in 1990—all of them are interlocking. This means that, once you have the puzzles in a standing position, you can pick them up by any piece and turn them completely around without having them fall apart. But, you have to make sure you keep them vertical and don't tip them!

The first project I cut out when I brought home that wonderful new toy, my first scroll saw, was a three-piece rabbit. As a woodworker of long standing, I used lumber I had in my workshop. It was an old piece of 1" x 4" pine. One of the things I liked about the puzzle was that it was thick enough to stand. The concept of a "freestanding" puzzle stayed with me as I moved on to using hardwoods.

Why animals?

Like everyone else I know who bought a scroll saw, I started not with my own designs but with patterns in the public domain from library books. I then traced the patterns onto the boards—which often took longer than cutting them out!

The first few original designs I did were of dinosaurs. But one can only design so many of anything before monotony sets in. I did three elephant patterns and then designed the Mama Rabbit with Babies puzzle (See the in-process photos in this book, page 9.).

Deciding what to design next got easier once I started selling my puzzles. That's because people told me what their interests were. (If you're going to design a new puzzle, you might as well design one that people are more likely to want to buy.) People asked for animal puzzles, which reinforced my own interest in them. My own interests combined with my customers' requests made a powerful reason for designing new animal puzzles.

Why hardwoods?

1. They're naturally beautiful. As a "lover" of hardwoods, I have a natural aversion to painting them. They're beautiful in their own right. Besides that, hardwoods occur naturally in a wide variety of colors. Why cut a tiger out of a piece of pine and then paint it when you can cut it from a tiger-colored wood complete with stripes? But more about that later.

2. The harder the wood, the less chip-out you get. The structure of hardwoods appears to be more uniform. Uniform density makes your cutting more consistent. You'll spend less time overall and end up with a more pleasing result.

3. The increased density also results in a surface that can be more easily sanded smooth. To paraphrase something we said in our first two books, *Dinosaur Puzzles for the Scroll Saw* and *Fantasy & Legend Puzzles for the Scroll Saw*: silky translates into sales at an art show.

Where can you buy hardwoods?

Look in the yellow pages of your phone book under "Lumber, Hardwood." Ask your woodworking friends. Check out the ads in your favorite scroll sawing or woodworking magazine; some of these magazines may be available at your local library, specialty woodworking retailers, or hobby shop. Keep your eyes open as you drive through unfamiliar areas. We're on the road a lot driving to and from shows. We found one of our best and most reliable suppliers in Ohio that way. If you have access to the Internet, use a search engine to find "Hardwood Lumber Dealers."

For more information about wood, your local public library is a source that's available to everyone. If you have a home computer, the door to almost unlimited information is open to you. This is especially true if you also have access to the Internet. Here are a few of the resources available to those with access to computers and the Internet:

www.windsorplywood.com – An amazing site, giving information on the wood from hundreds of different trees.

www.woodworkerssource.net – This is the Website for a hardwood dealer in Arizona. The site offers information about many hardwoods. I have found this dealer to be an excellent and reliable source for much of the exotic lumber I buy.

How do I choose wood for color and cutting characteristics?

I try to choose woods suitable for the item being cut. For instance, polar bears only come in white, so I always cut them from aspen. I also pay attention to my customers. Moose almost always sell best in black walnut. Evidently most people think that's the right color for Moose.

Almost every puzzle has a wood in which it sells best. I know that I might not have found the perfect wood for a particular pattern yet, and that knowledge keeps me searching for new and wonderful woods.

Most of my puzzles are cut in native North American hardwoods. Cherry, walnut, and maple are widely available in this area. Cherry appears to be the wood of choice (at the moment), but walnut is gaining in popularity.

Maple is less popular because many parents don't want to buy light-colored toys for small children. I also use a smaller amount of butternut, aspen, and catalpa. These woods are locally available in limited quantities.

From time to time, I use sweet gum, mesquite, sassafras, and other regionally-grown woods. All of these woods have advantages and disadvantages. Many truly beautiful woods are too hard (or almost too hard) to cut with a scroll saw. Most of these types are exotics. When I run across a new species, I pick up a board. If it's heavier than a similar-sized board of hard maple, I put it back.

I always look at every board I buy. I'm looking for color and figure. I want the richest color for that species and any figure I can find— wavy, quilted, fiddleback, etc. (You will need to learn "Lumberspeak." See the tip box on page 15.) I also like the contrast between heartwood and sapwood. (See the gallery photo of the dolphin on page 51.) While you're at it, contrast the finished item with the photo of the dolphin with carrier prior to drum sanding. (See the photo on page 15.)

What are some of the advantages and disadvantages of various hardwoods?

The biggest disadvantage of hardwoods is price. Most hardwoods are more expensive than most softwoods. However, if you're using hardwoods, you don't have to buy 87 kinds of paint, learn to paint, or spend the time painting your projects.

The biggest advantage of hardwoods is beauty. With careful selection, you can produce a really good-looking puzzle.

There is one characteristic of hardwoods that's both an advantage and a disadvantage: the hardness. It takes longer to cut a puzzle in hardwood, but the finished piece is stronger. This is a great selling point for children's toys (and for puzzles for clumsy adults).

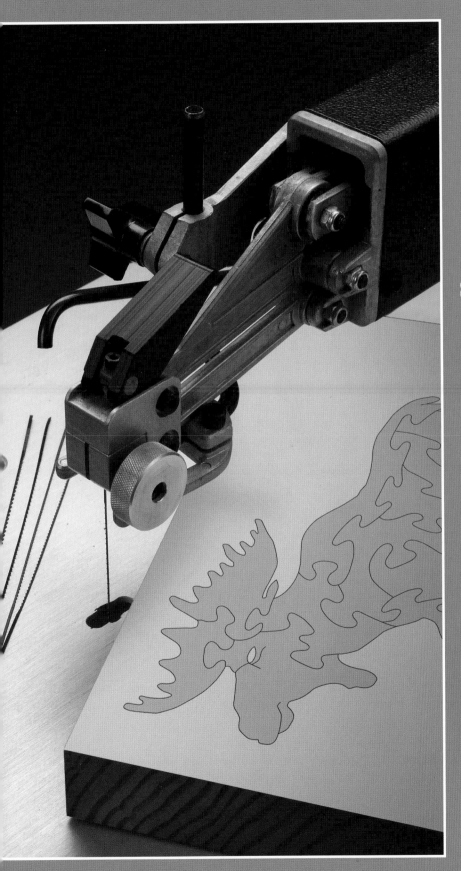

1

Getting Started

Safety

It should come as no surprise that cutting thick wood generates a lot of sawdust. Nor should it come as a surprise that breathing sawdust is not good for you. In my workshop, I have a dust collector and an air cleaner. The dust collector picks up the large particles and many of the small ones. Even if you have a dust collector, however, the air in your workshop will still have lots of tiny particles floating around. My air cleaner is mounted on the ceiling and removes a high percentage of the particles that the dust collector misses. Beyond using those two machines, I wear a dust mask that uses replaceable filters.

Eye protection is a must! I was in fifth grade when I got my first pair of glasses. Because I can't find a company that makes the kind of safety glasses I want and because I can't see well enough to work without my regular glasses, I use my regular glasses for much of my woodworking. However, my regular glasses have titanium frames and hardened lenses. When I'm sanding, I wear side shields. These translucent plastic devices slide onto your frames and keep flying particles from hitting your eyes from the side. They are available at most vision centers. Whatever type of eye protection you use in your workshop should include side shielding. If you don't need prescription lenses, use safety goggles.

You'll also do a better job of cutting and be safer if your saw has a good, efficient dust blower. This device, of course, blows the dust away from your cut line. I call this a safety issue because, before I had a blower, I reached up without thinking, to wipe the dust away from the cut line, and cut myself! Don't let it happen to you.

Also make sure to have enough light in your workshop to see what you're doing. I have two swing-arm lamps (widely available anywhere lamps are sold) mounted on my saw. These lamps come with clamps, and you can usually find somewhere to attach them if you don't have a mount for them on your saw. I find I can cut longer with light coming from both sides. This setup also eliminates shadows and a good amount of eyestrain. You need adequate light for everything else you do in the workshop, too.

I also wear a hearing protector. If you're into serious woodworking, you would be well advised to at least invest in a mask, eye protection, some type of hearing protection, and possibly a dust collector.

Figure 1.1
Squaring the Blade with an Engineer's Square.

A word about saws

I have owned four different brands of saws and have used several others. Although it's easier to cut anything with a great, big, expensive, production-quality saw, all of these patterns have been cut with a cheap, rickety, difficult machine. Just keep practicing.

I have never seen a saw with a truly accurate degree gauge. Be sure your table is square to the blade; get an engineer's square and use it to level the table. Check your squareness if you have trouble cutting a true vertical.

To check that the blade is square to the table, lift the saw arm up as far as it will go and place the square next to the blade. Place a white piece of paper behind it to allow yourself to see the blade and the edge of the square as clearly as possible. (See Figure 1.1.) If the edge of the square is not perfectly parallel to the blade, your table is not level. Adjust the table accordingly.

You may also want to check that the blade is moving in a true or nearly true up-and-down motion. Steve Malavolta wrote a great tip in his "Layered Marquetry Puzzles" article in the Spring 2005 issue of *Scroll Saw Workshop*. He suggests moving the blade to the "up" position, and then placing a flat piece of material next to the blade. Slowly move the blade to the down position and watch to see if the blade gets closer or farther away to the material. If the blade doesn't move, you're in good shape. If it does move side to side, use your saw adjustments (if your saw has them) or try shimming at the blade clamps as necessary. I adjusted my blade after reading Steve's tip and I am getting better cuts.

Cutting on the line

Cutting on the line is fairly important on the outer edges of the puzzle. It is very important for facial features and is sometimes important on the inner cuts.

If you wobble on the outside edge of a puzzle, you can either re-cut it or ignore it. If you get off the line while cutting any of the features, stop. Look at where you are and see if the cut can be saved. If it can, try to do so. If it can't, throw the puzzle out and try again.

PARTS OF THE KEY

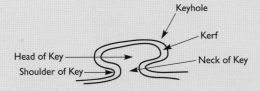

Figure 1.2. Parts of a Key.

On the interior (or interlocking) cuts, accuracy is not terribly important. What is important is the shape of the key. In order for the key not to pull out of the keyhole, the head of the key must be larger than the neck of the key. It also must be balanced so that there is material on both sides of the neck.

On puzzles with large pieces, there is a lot of room for error. The smaller and more complex the pieces, the more important accuracy is. See Figure 1.2, which shows how to cut the key, as well as how it is designed.

Preventing burn marks

Burn marks are a frequent problem when cutting light-colored hardwoods. After gluing the pattern in place, cover the pattern with a clear plastic sealing tape. The heat generated by the friction of the saw blade causes the plastic tape to melt. This lubricates the cut and almost eliminates burn marks.

Clear plastic sealing tape is available at department stores, office supply stores, grocery stores, and lumberyards, just to name a few. You want 2" clear plastic tape without the Mylar strands. By following this tip, I can even cut purpleheart without leaving (many) burn marks.

I cut this cherry puzzle without covering the pattern with 2" plastic tape. This piece is external, so I had quite a bit of sanding to do to get rid of the burn mark.

Pattern classifications

Three-dimensional puzzles are much more difficult for young children than flat puzzles with the same number of pieces. With three-dimensional puzzles, there are small muscle control issues involved. That's why I advise people not to give a more complicated puzzle to a young child. Also note that most of the puzzles in this book contain swallowable pieces! It is critical that none of those puzzles are within the reach of children under the age of three. Here's the easy way to tell: if a piece will pass through the hole in a roll of bathroom tissue, the piece is swallowable.

Easy – The puzzles marked "easy" have fewer pieces and uncomplicated faces. The Golden Retriever has seven pieces and a happy face.

Intermediate – These puzzles have more detail cuts in addition to the facial features.

Advanced – Most of these puzzles have complicated faces, which demand a great deal of control.

Mama Rabbit with Babies.
Butternut, approximately 7" high.

2

Cutting a Mama Rabbit with Babies
Step-by-Step

I teach scroll sawing at my local Woodcraft store. Many of my students are just getting started, so I developed a practice pattern for them. (See page 29.) Maybe you'll want practice before you tackle some of the patterns in this book. If so, copy the pattern, glue it to a piece of scrap lumber, and practice away!

Before you can cut a puzzle out, of course, you must select the board you want to use. Examine the board carefully both top and bottom, looking for bad spots, including checks, knotholes, and obvious internal cracks. Mark these flaws on the top of your board. I use a wide, black permanent marker for this task.

Make a copy of the Mama Rabbit with Babies pattern and decide where to position it on the board. Avoid the bad spots when positioning your pattern. Spray the pattern with repositionable spray adhesive and apply the pattern to the board.

Be sure the adhesive you choose is "repositionable." If the label on a product doesn't include that word, you don't want to use that product for this purpose. The bond from a non-repositionable adhesive will be so secure that you'll have to spend time sanding the pattern off the pieces. However, patterns glued with repositionable spray adhesive peel off leaving no residue. (Hint: The longer you wait to peel the pattern off, the harder it will be to do so.) I've had good luck with Duro All-Purpose Spray Adhesive, available at K-Mart and Wal-Mart stores, as well as many lumberyards.

As you probably know, scroll saw blades come in sizes from 2 through 12. The lower the number, the finer the teeth. If the board you're using for this puzzle is 5/4", you'll need a #9 blade. If your board is 4/4" or slightly less, use a #7 blade.

Tools and Supplies

Scroll saw with dust blower
#9 or #7 skip tooth or reverse tooth blades
Repositionable spray adhesive
Square
Clear 2" packing tape
Disk pad
Drill with variable speed lock
Drill stand
Sanding disks
Flap sander
Flat trays
Glue box

Metal tray
Paper towels
Plastic bags, gallon (resealable)
Rubber gloves
Rubber finger tips
Board of appropriate dimensions and 7/8" to 1 1/4" thick
1/4" burr bit
Additional supplies needed for the frame tray puzzle
Baltic birch boards (1/4" thick) of the appropriate size
A board of contrasting color (3/8" thick) of same size as the birch

Enlarge 110%

GRAIN

1 I try to lay out (and glue down) enough patterns to fill an entire board. This maximizes my wood use while minimizing my scrap.

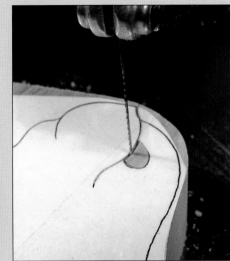

2 Start cutting at the tip of the nose. Cut through the base of the eye, back up, and cut out the eye piece. Back out past the tip of the nose, turn around, and start down the nose. Do the mouth cut, back out, and continue around the base of the rabbit.

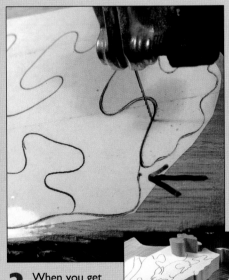

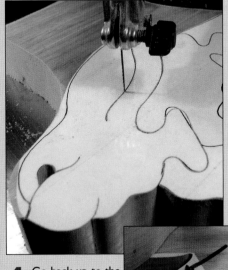

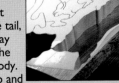

3 When you get around to the tail, cut a short way up between the tail and the body. Then, back up and turn around in the waste, as indicated by the arrow. Go around the rest of the tail and cut it free.

4 Go back up to the neck to cut the head and ears free. Make the dividing cut between the ears, back out, and turn around in the waste, as indicated by the arrow.

5 Starting again at the mama's neck, cut down and along the base of the baby. Make the front and hind leg detail cuts in the baby while you have large pieces to hang on to. This makes the cutting much easier. Cut the base piece free.

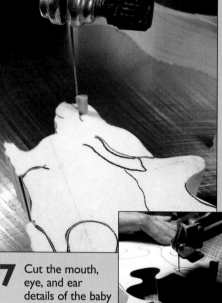

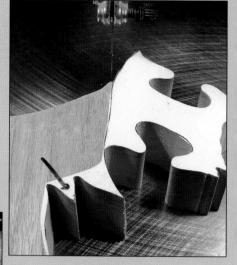

6 Start at the tip of the baby's front foot, and cut around the front of the baby. Cut the first top piece of the mama free.

7 Cut the mouth, eye, and ear details of the baby as you go.

8 Cut the last two pieces free.

Cutting the babies

When I first designed the Mama Rabbit with Babies puzzle, I was using ⁴⁄₄" stock. The puzzle looked as it does today, except it had only one baby, cut into three pieces. (See Figure 2.1)

The puzzle was an instant success, but there was a potential problem. A lot of people were buying this puzzle as a baby shower gift. An infant might put of one of the small pieces in his or her mouth and choke. I thought about it, decided to go to a ⁵⁄₄" board, and turned the baby into triplets. Substituting two cuts one way for two the other resulted in a more realistic puzzle. It also eliminated a potentially serious problem. The moral is, when you start designing your own puzzles, keep your eyes and ears open. You can solve problems, but only if you recognize them for what they are.

To turn one baby into three, follow the step-by-step instructions on page 11.

Figure 2.1 The baby bunny was originally cut into a mini three-piece puzzle, but these pieces were not child safe. Therefore, I started slicing the baby bunny lengthwise.

1 Divide the baby piece lengthwise into two or three slices. (I can eyeball twins, but I always measure and mark for triplets.) This depends on the thickness of the board. This board was ⁵⁄₄" butternut. That is, it was 1¼" actual thickness. The square I use is marked in millimeters (mm). I marked the board (in three places) to make the two outside bunnies each 11 mm wide and the middle one 10 mm.

2 Cut the first baby free.

3 Cut the remainder of the baby in half.

4 The last two babies are separated.

5 The cutting is done.

Cutting a Mama Rabbit with Babies

Sanding your puzzle

There are two reasons to sand your puzzle (or any other project). The first is to correct mistakes in cutting. With puzzles, the most common problem is that the pieces stick. This is remedied by careful sanding of the head of the key and of the shoulders of the keyhole. Sand lightly and test the fit. It's easy to overdo it.

The second reason to sand is to improve the surface of your puzzle. I do a three-step sanding process: 1) sand the top and bottom of each piece, 2) check the cut surfaces for smoothness and gently touch up any rough spots, and 3) round over all of the edges. This process gives a professional finish to each puzzle.

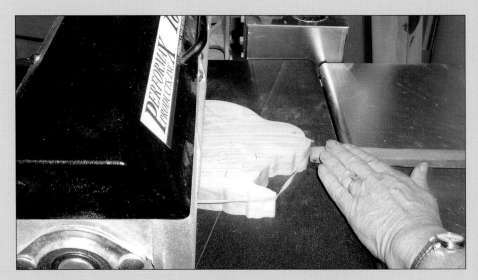

1 I like to sand the top and bottom of each piece using a drum sander. However, you can use a 5" disk sanding pad (220 grit) chucked into a drill secured by a drill stand. I used to do all of my flat sanding this way before we invested in the drum sander. Simply be careful to keep the flat sides level as you sand, and wear finger protection (See Step 4, on the next page). The only problem I've had using the disk sander in this way is occasionally sanding a piece unevenly. You will improve with practice. The top and bottom surfaces can also be sanded with an orbital or a pad sander. Rubber band the puzzle together for stability and sand away. If you have a drum sander, see the tip box on the next page for more information.

Sanding Techniques

I use a flap sander to round off the sharp edges of my puzzles. This also provides visual definition to the interior pieces. I bought my first Sand-O-Flex flap sander about 1970. At the time, I was refinishing furniture. The Sand-O-Flex was developed specifically for sanding chair rungs, and other similar items, without gouging them.

When I began cutting jigsaw puzzles and I wanted something to round off the edges, the Sand-O-Flex was ideal.

To purchase the Sand-O-Flex and supplies, try Key Abrasives, 800–634–4748, **www.key-abrasive.presys.com**, or contact Merit Abrasives, 800–421–1936, **www.meritabrasives.com**, for a distributor near you.

2 After sanding the top and bottom of each puzzle piece, I check the cut surfaces for smoothness. Touch up any rough places—gently—to keep the fit.

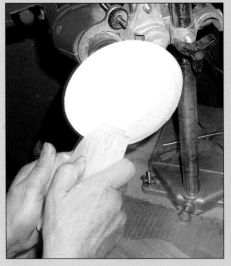

3 I use the disk sander to sand all of the outer edges of each puzzle. Any part that someone is likely to touch should be smooth.

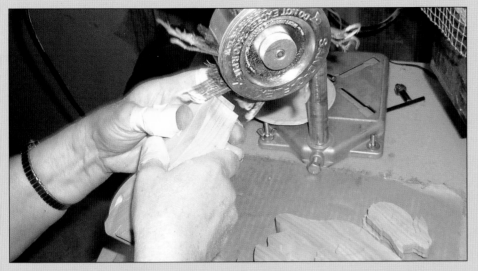

4 My last step is to round over all of the edges. Notice the rubber finger protectors. Without them, you can take the skin off your fingers so fast! Rubber finger tips are available in several sizes at office supply stores. Rounding over the edges gives a nice finish, provides visual separation of the pieces, and sometime removes a flaw. I use a Sand-O-Flex flap sander. This gadget was designed to round over edges without gouging. I use a 240-grit scored refill and cut along the scored lines. I end up with 64 ⅛" strips of sandpaper, which can get into all the little places in the puzzle pieces. You can adjust the length of the strips for larger and smaller pieces.

5 Here the mama rabbit has been partly Sand-O-Flexed.

6 Use the disc sander to sand the baby rabbits. Remember, only the top and bottom surface of the one-piece baby went through the drum sander. Now that we've cut the baby into three pieces, four more baby sides need to be flat sanded. I use my disc sander for this purpose.

Using a drum sander

I find that using a drum sander has cut my sanding time by 60%. If you have a relatively good surface to begin with, you can sand with only a finish grit. I usually use a 220- or 180-grit belt.

Note: There are puzzles that I cannot put through the drum sander without breaking them. I've placed a "drum sander" symbol (⚙) on the patterns in the pattern section (page 27) that can be sanded with the drum sander. You can use a drum sander on all of the patterns provided that you save the scrap and use it as a carrier. The patterns marked with the ⚙ symbol go through with only a rubber band around them.

To use a drum sander to sand your puzzles, follow the steps below:

Rubber band the puzzle to prepare for drum sanding.

• Put a rubber band completely around the outside of each puzzle. Rubber band size #64 works for most of the puzzles in this book. (See the photo above.)

• If you're doing several puzzles, group them by how thick the wood is.

• Start with the group made of the thickest wood.

• Position each puzzle on the conveyor belt so that it goes through with the grain (otherwise the drum will leave visible marks).

• Run the first group through on both sides. Use one or more push sticks to support each puzzle as it goes through.

• Adjust the height of the sanding drum for the next group.

You'll have to experiment with this process. Start with some of the simpler puzzles to get the hang of it.

Finishing

Note: All of the oil and stain products recommended in this book are volatile and hazardous if not used carefully. Read and follow (but do not be cowed by) label instructions! Because I usually want the actual wood colors to come through, I use Danish Oil Natural to finish my puzzles. I've had good luck with the General Finishes brand.

In the first edition of this book (published in 2005), I recommended using a clear UV-blocking Danish oil on exotic woods. However, I stopped using that oil in 2006. In my experience, the chemical composition of this oil makes drying a problem. I had to spend more time rubbing than I was willing to do.

Because making and selling puzzles is my business, I do a lot of oiling. I start by pouring the oil into a one-gallon, resealable freezer bag. Next, I disassemble the puzzle and drop the pieces into the oil. I let them sit in the oil for a short time, and then remove them from the oil. As soon as they're out of the bag of oil, I place them on plastic trays lined with paper towels to air dry.

Dipping your hands directly into the oil (or the stain, as we shall see later) to retrieve the pieces would be messy and hard on your hands. I recommend that you use gloves made of nitrile, rather than latex—experience has taught me that oil dissolves latex! You can buy nitrile gloves at any woodworking, medical, or beauty supply store.

Most of the pieces dry completely without wiping, but I inspect all the pieces and wipe as necessary. The more cut line detail there is in a puzzle piece, the more attention it needs at this step. This is because more oil gets into the cut line than can be absorbed by the surfaces internal to any given cut. Then it bleeds out, usually over several hours. This tends to be more of a problem with the very dense, tight-grained exotics—especially satinwood and chakte kok. I oil those woods first, and inspect them periodically as I'm oiling the rest of the

batch. Usually, by the time I'm done with the batch, those pieces are dry. After drying any of the pieces that need it, I assemble the puzzles and let them air-dry overnight.

Remember, oil fumes are extremely volatile. I dry the pieces on paper towels because they dry quickly and completely. I dispose of them by dropping them <u>loosely</u> into a large paper bag and letting them dry overnight. This permits no buildup of fumes to cause spontaneous combustion. The important thing is <u>not</u> to stuff them tightly into a plastic bag or any airtight container.

To create a black finish on certain puzzles, such as the Holstein cow on page 78 and the Penguin on page 68, I stain the required pieces using Behlen's Jet Black stain first. After dipping and letting the pieces dry overnight, I assemble each puzzle to make sure I've got the right pieces together. I then disassemble each puzzle and oil all the pieces of the same cow together. I try very hard to oil all the pieces of the same puzzle at the same time. However, oiling the pieces of more than one puzzle at once leads to trouble—which pieces go with which puzzle?

Using a carrier with a drum sander

I often use a carrier, made of the scrap wood I've cut away from the puzzle. To do this, I save the scrap pieces, fit them back around the puzzle, rubber band them together, and run them through with everything else. For non-landscape puzzles, I refer to the scrap pieces, which I assemble together with the actual puzzle pieces, as the "carrier." The carrier helps to avoid crunching the puzzles.

Lumberspeak

- **Grain Figures.** "Figured," "fiddleback," "quilted," "wavy," "flame crotch," etc. are terms that really mean that the grain of the wood is not straight.

- **Hardwood and softwood.** "Hardwood" only means "deciduous tree," or a tree that loses its leaves in the fall. It has nothing to do with how hard the wood is. Some hardwoods are softer (less dense, lighter) than some softwoods.

- **Maple and oak.** Lumber people know only two kinds of maple, hard and soft, and only two kinds of oak, red and white. This is the case regardless of the fact that there are 20 or 30 species of each.

- **Hardwood sizes.** Hardwoods are sold by the quarter inch, i.e., ¾" (three-quarter), ⁵⁄₄" (five-quarter), etc. This is the unplaned measurement. Planing reduces the thickness of the board. If you go to specialty lumberyards, they will plane to your specifications, for a price.

- **Skip planing.** Hardwood lumber dealers will usually skip plane your lumber if you ask them to do so. This type of planing will give you the thickest board possible. However, you will have to pay more attention when you sand to make sure everything is smooth.

- **Kerf.** This refers to the wood taken out by the saw blade.

Mama Rabbit with Babies and Bunny puzzles.
Back row: Mama Rabbit with Babies. Butternut, approximately 7" high.
Front row: Bunny (from left to right) in beech, ash, lacewood, and
aspen, each approximately 4" high. What a difference wood makes!

3

Adapting a Pattern

From Mama Rabbit with Babies to four-piece Bunny

The rabbit pattern changed yet again when customers wanted a simpler, less expensive puzzle for children. I reduced the outline of the mama rabbit and added the puzzle cuts for the bunny. (See Figure 3.1.) The sanding and finishing instructions covered in Chapter 2, pages 12 to 14, apply.

From four-piece Bunny to Easy Bunny

It changed again when I altered the Bunny puzzle cuts to the shaped keys, creating the Easy Bunny. (See Figure 3.2.) I do relatively few of these puzzles. It's only suitable for children under the age of two. I do other puzzles in an easy format as my whimsy takes me. I cut a little clear plastic template, which I put over an existing pattern, and trace over the existing keys with a colored pen. (See Figure 3.3.) I used this method on a seven-piece brown bear puzzle, effectively changing it into a four-piece puzzle, suitable for two- and three-year-olds. (See Figure 3.4.)

Figure 3.1: I created the *Bunny* pattern on the right by reducing the *Mama Rabbit with Babies* pattern (above).

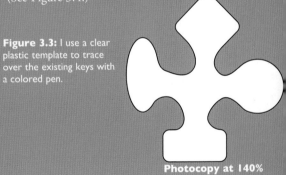

Figure 3.3: I use a clear plastic template to trace over the existing keys with a colored pen.

Photocopy at 140%

Figure 3.2: The *Easy Bunny* pattern features differently shaped keys.

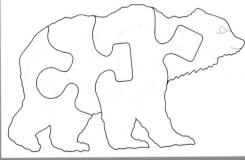

Figure 3.4: This seven-piece *Brown Bear* puzzle is changed into a four-piece puzzle using the clear plastic template.

Bunny

Easy Bunny

Photocopy at 110%

Mama Rabbit Frame Tray.
Baltic birch (frame tray) and mahogany (rabbit), approximately 7" high.

Figure 3.5: The pieces in a frame tray puzzle don't need to have keys to interlock them; the frame keeps the pieces in place.

From Mama Rabbit with Babies to a frame tray puzzle

The latest adaptation is to turn Mama Rabbit with Babies into a frame tray puzzle. The process of adapting the rabbit is the same as before. Reduce the outline of the mama rabbit. Draw in the puzzle cut lines. These pieces don't need to have keys to interlock them; the frame will keep them in place.

Looking at Figure 3.5, you can see I used two different woods for the puzzle. The frame and the backing are Baltic birch plywood. I use Baltic birch because it's good on both sides (no flaws), all the plies are birch (there is no

softwood core), and it has no voids (holes in the interior plies).

The rabbit is mahogany and is thicker than the frame. It isn't really necessary to use two different woods. I like the contrast, but you can stain or paint for a similar result.

Note that the pattern you see in the in-process photos (pages 21 and 22) is not the pattern of the finished item. With the way the pieces were originally drawn, a child could have swallowed one of them, so I altered the design as I was cutting.

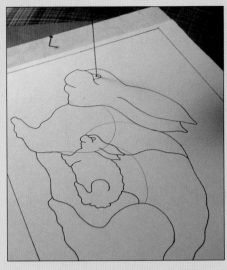

1 To use two boards for the frame and the rabbit, tack or tape the two boards together. I used tacks for this project.

2 Drill an access hole in the rabbit's eye. Insert the blade through the access hole, and cut the eye shape. Discard the scrap.

3 Cut outward from the eye to the tip of the nose, down and around to the ears.

4 Cut down between the ears, back out, and make a tight turn (as indicated by the arrow in the inset photo).

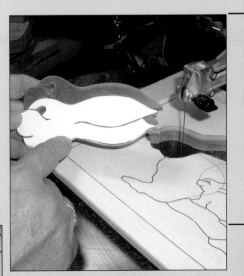

5 Cut around the second ear and down to the starting point. Remove the head.

Backing Out

Most of the cut line detail I use involves cutting in and backing out of that cut. It takes some practice, but the trick is to relax. Pull gently back along your cut line, and don't try to over-control the direction. There are several spots on the practice pattern for you to try backing out.

Blade Tension

You have to experiment with your saw to learn how to and how much to adjust the tension. I usually readjust the tension when I change sizes or types of blade.

6 Cut the rest of the pieces out, removing each as you free it. At this point, you have two puzzles and two frames (if you used two different woods). If you used one board, you have one of each. Set the rabbit aside.

7 Do any surface sanding on the frame and the backer board at this point. Be sure to sand both sides of the backer because the inside will show when the rabbit is removed. Next, glue the frame to the backer board (I use Elmer's Carpenter's Glue) and clamp the two together overnight.

8 After the glue has dried, return to the saw and trim the frame and backer board together. Trimming after they're glued is the easiest way to keep them straight. Sand the rabbit pieces and the edges of the frame as usual. I usually wipe oil on the frame tray. Dip the rabbit pieces as described in the Finishing section of Chapter 2 on page 14. Let them dry thoroughly, and give the completed puzzle to a small child.

Designing a Puzzle from a Photograph

When I decided to add dogs to the puzzle line, we started carrying our new digital camera wherever we went. This is a picture of Sophie, a Sheltie who lives down the street and around the corner. (See Figure 4.1.) She was only seven months old at this time and was very bouncy.

Dave cropped and enlarged the photo on our computer and printed it in black and white on plain paper. Next, I traced over the figure of the dog. (See Figure 4.2.) I realized she was standing at an angle to the camera (and to me). To make all four of the dog's feet touch ground, I had to give her a stand. I liked the look of the patio blocks on which she was standing. I decided to use detail cuts to make the stand look like a patio.

I design what I think of as vaguely anatomical puzzles. I tried to show the fluffiness of the dog's coat with zigzag lines. I decided to make the face and the ruff into separate pieces as well as all four legs, the body, and the tail. I needed to make the tail more distinct, so I stole some of the rear hip and added a little bulk to the outside of the tail. I also curved the tip of the tail away from the leg. I added very triangular shapes for the puzzle keys to match the zigzag coat lines. (See Figure 4.3.) Dave scanned the newly created pattern into the computer, printed two copies, and I went to the saw.

Figure 4.1: Sophie, a Sheltie on our street.

When I actually sat down to cut the puzzle, I just couldn't face cutting all of those zigzags I had so carefully drawn. So I took my pencil and simplified the hair directly on the pattern, which was already glued to the board. Now, while this first cut puzzle was similar to the photo of the dog, I wasn't really happy with it. (See Figure 4.4.)

I narrowed the ruff and lengthened the muzzle. I also simplified and curved the puzzle keys. I changed the angle of the hair cuts and made them different lengths. With those changes, I thought I was done and drew a clean copy of the pattern, scanned it, and cut a new puzzle.

But I wasn't done. At an art show, I met a Sheltie breeder and asked her to criticize the puzzle. She did and I changed the line of the dog's back. So with version three (or is it four?) I think it's done. See the final pattern, Figure 4.5.

While the details will differ from project to project, the preceding account is pretty representative of the events that occur in designing a new puzzle. I usually end up doing at least three versions of a new pattern.

We make it sound almost as if a computer is required to design new patterns. In fact, it is not. Having a computer makes it easier, but before we acquired one, I got along without it. I just made a lot of trips to the copy shop!

Figure 4.2: Tracing over the figure of the dog.

Figure 4.3: I created triangular-shaped keys to match the zigzag coat lines.

Figure 4.4: The first puzzle I cut was similar to the photo of the dog, but it wasn't quite what I wanted.

Figure 4.5: The final pattern and puzzle.

5

Designing Facial Expressions

The facial expression on your little wooden animal often determines its appeal. Babyish faces are appealing in large part because of the size of the eyes. Most of these animals have eyes that are much larger, relative to the head, than they are in real life. Many also have an eyebrow cut that enhances the expression of the eyes.

In addition to the eye cuts, most patterns have a mouth cut ranging from a simple slit to a more complicated shape. The mouths on most of my puzzle patterns are curved up slightly. I learned long ago that frowns don't look good on little wooden animal faces. Some patterns even have a little nostril cut. These are the details that give personality to the designs. Cut all of the details before you cut the entire piece free of the board.

I've grouped the patterns in this book by category (pets, wildlife, etc.). Within each category, the puzzles' difficulties are noted. In most cases, the difficulty is related to the facial features.

The simplest type of eye is the one in the rabbits: two curved lines that meet on each end and form a curved hole. (See Figure 5.1.) Adding an eyebrow doesn't make it much harder. (See Figure 5.2.)

The other simple eye involves drilling a hole at the appropriate place in the head. This is what I've done with the animals in the puzzle

Figure 5.1: The simplest eye is two curved lines that meet on each end and form a curved hole.

Figure 5.2: Adding an eyebrow gives the eye interest without making it too difficult to cut.

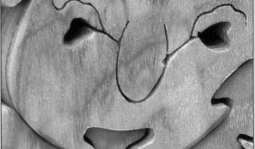

Figure 5.4: The *Bulldog* and *Koala Twins* puzzles have complicated facial features to capture their expressions. Use caution when you are scrolling these areas.

Figure 5.3: You can detail a drilled eye with a teardrop-shaped burr in a rotary power tool.

Noah's Ark. A word of warning—drill the holes before you cut the item. When drilling close to a cut edge with a tiny drill bit, the bit has a tendency to wander. If you don't have a drill press, don't try to drill the eyes on the animals in the ark. There's no room for error, and it looks fine without the eyes anyway.

For animals for which it's appropriate, the next step for a drilled eye is to detail it with a teardrop-shaped burr in a rotary power tool. I recommend the teardrop shape because you can vary the depth and therefore the diameter of the eye socket. Figure 5.3 shows the use of this burr on the dolphin. I used the same burr for the elephant as well.

Another variation is to drill an access hole and cut the eye(s) from it. The Persian Cat is done that way. It has the further complication of a drilled and cut mouth shape.

The two puzzles in this book with the most complicated faces are the Bulldog and the Koala Twins. With the Bulldog, you have to decide in what sequence to make the cuts. Cut the details in the nosepiece first and remove it. Next, cut all of the head details that you can without releasing it from the board. After cutting the head free, you'll still have one detail cut to make. Be careful where you place your fingers to guide the wood through those last few cuts. It's possible to break some of those fragile pieces.

The faces on the koala puzzle are even more complicated. Cut in from the left and cut out the left eye. Then cut over to the nose line; cut down, around, and up the right side, back down a trifle, and cut into the right eye. Cut out the right eye detail. Back around the nose and into the left eye; then back into the bottom of the nose, and cut the little upstroke. This is easier (and faster) to do than to describe.

6

The Puzzle Patterns

On the following pages, you'll find a selection of my animal patterns. The patterns are grouped by category, but I have also given them an easy, intermediate, and advanced rating as well. I've also included a landscape puzzle. Using the techniques outlined in this book, you can modify them to suit your particular style or purpose. For example, you can simplify the advanced puzzles if you want to give a specific puzzle to a young child.

The Puzzle Patterns

Grain and Color Considerations

One of the most important things to consider when you lay out a puzzle is the grain direction. If you lay out your puzzle so that the long, thin pieces are with the grain, those pieces will be stronger. I've included grain arrows on the patterns to show the direction in which I usually lay out the puzzles. Look at the *Dolphin* on page 51. I laid it out with the long, thin tail pieces with the grain. Some puzzles, like the *Elephant* on page 45, can be laid out in any direction, because the pieces are all fairly thick. Many of the patterns in this book can be tilted at 15 or 20 degrees from the grain arrows without problems.

If the puzzle does not have any fragile pieces, you can lay out the pieces to take advantage of a particularly beautiful grain pattern. This is what I did with the *Golden Retriever* (page 33).

Besides grain direction and grain pattern, another thing I consider as I create puzzles is color. The subject often dictates the species and/or color of wood for a particular animal. For instance, polar bears need to be cut from a white wood, and Holsteins need to be black and white. Other choices are less obvious, and you just need to pay attention. For example, elephants sell better in cherry than in walnut, and tree frogs sell best in padauk. I don't know why, but they do.

People seem to like the heartwood/sapwood contrast found in many woods (again, see the *Elephant* on page 45 and the *Dolphin* on page 51). Items cut from bird's-eye maple (as well as any wood with figured grain, wormholes, resin pockets, and anything else unusual) are always popular.

Several years ago, I realized that some of my customers have a strong wood preference and may not know it. They will come to my booth at an art show and admire several items cut from the same wood. I will say something like, "You have a marked preference for bird's-eye maple." That comment will often result in a sale that may not otherwise have happened.

◑ = Drum sander safe
Patterns with this symbol can be put through the drum sander. All puzzles should be run through the drum sander with the grain. See the grain arrows on each pattern. See the tip box on page 13 for more information.

The Practice Pattern includes all of the techniques you need to know to cut any pattern in this book. Particularly useful are the lines where you have to cut in and back out. The tiny heads and keys are useful practice pieces for *Noah's Ark*. If you can cut all the shapes in the Practice Pattern, you can cut anything. So practice!

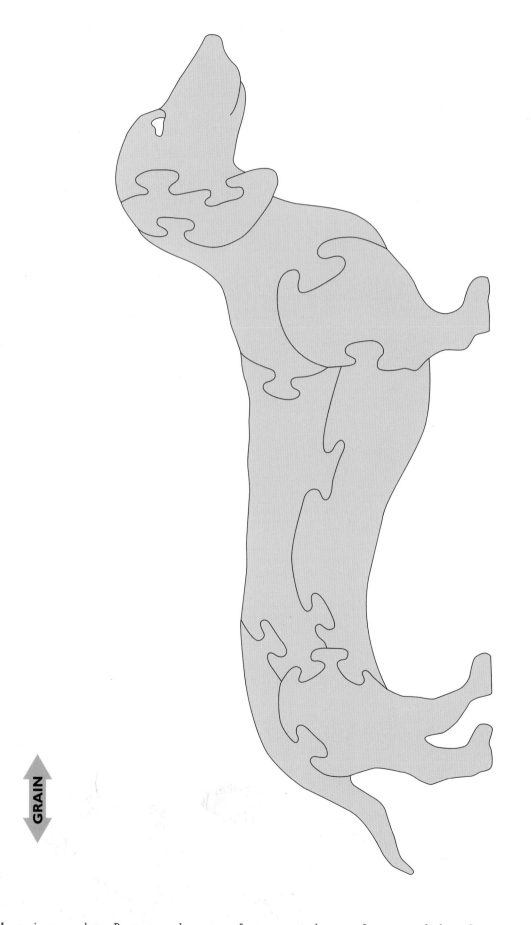

GRAIN

Photocopy at 100%

Dachshund

Birch, approximately 4" high.
First done for friends who named their dachsy "CD"
(short for "Compact Dog").

GRAIN

Photocopy at 100%

Cherry, approximately 5" high.
This is the little dog that won all of the shows in 2008.

GRAIN

OR

GRAIN

Photocopy at 100%

Cherry, approximately 6" high.
This is the dog we'd have if we weren't running
around to art shows all of the time.

GRAIN

Photocopy at 100%

Cherry, approximately 6" high.
Toto (from The Wizard of Oz) was a Cairn —in another color.

GRAIN

Photocopy at 100%

Walnut, approximately 6" high.
Lassie was a Collie, even if she was often a he of another color.

GRAIN

Photocopy at 100%

Bulldog

Walnut, approximately 7" high.
I love this face.

GRAIN

Photocopy at 100%

Bird's-eye maple, approximately 5" high.
Bird's eye maple makes a nice freckled cocker spaniel, but black is cute, too.

GRAIN

Photocopy at 100%

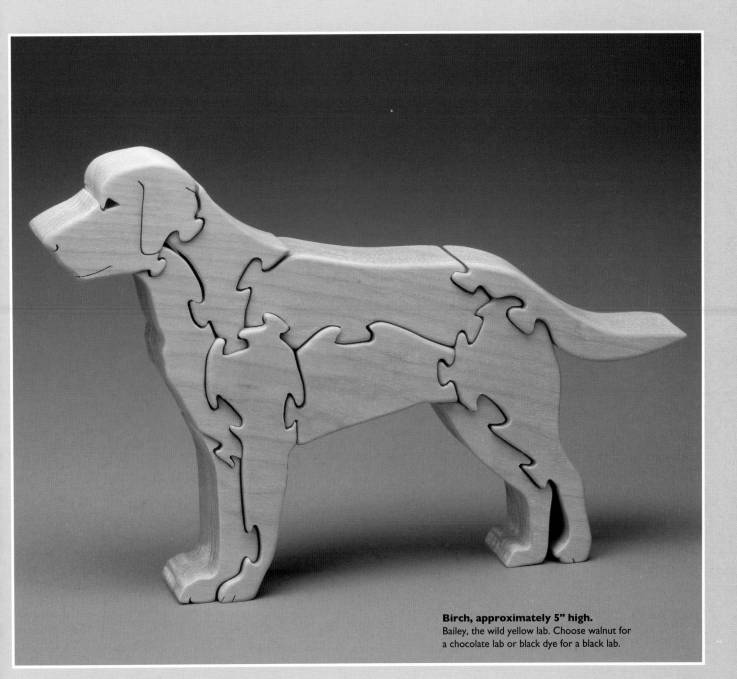

Birch, approximately 5" high.
Bailey, the wild yellow lab. Choose walnut for
a chocolate lab or black dye for a black lab.

GRAIN

Photocopy at 100

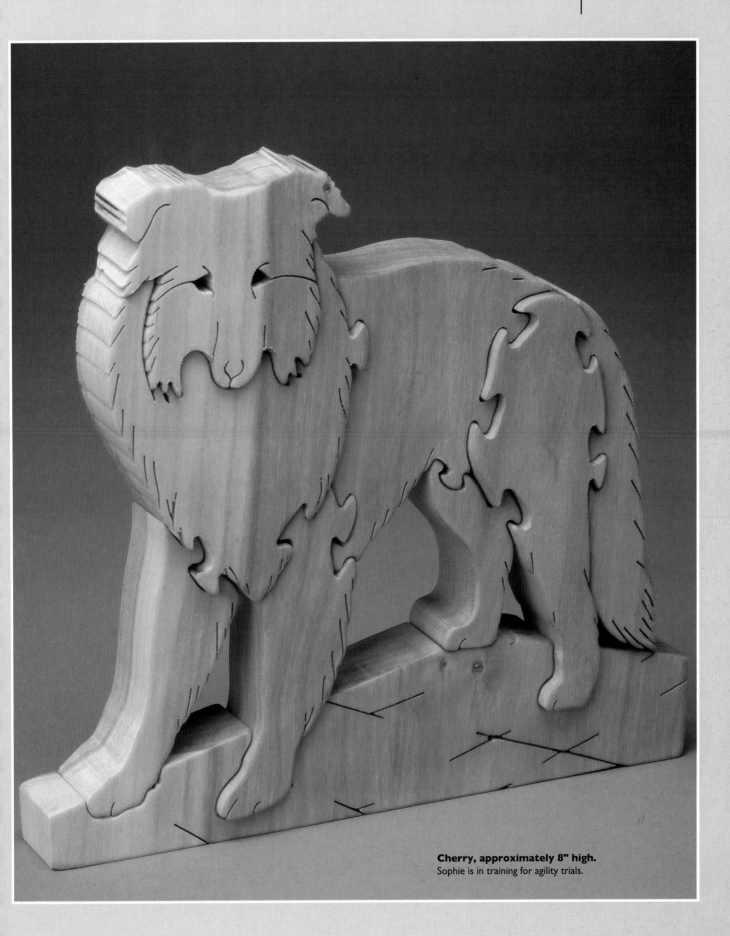

Cherry, approximately 8" high.
Sophie is in training for agility trials.

GRAIN

Photocopy at 100%

Cherry, approximately 6" high.
This is Breezy Marie Peterson, one of our grandkitties.

GRAIN

Photocopy at 100%

Persian Cat — Walking

Cherry, approximately 5" high.
Puss is our other grandkitty.

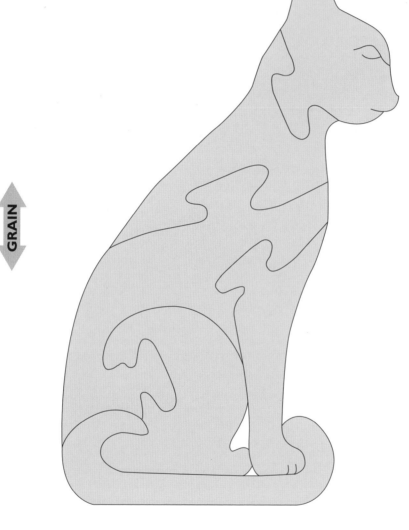

GRAIN

Photocopy at 100%

Bird's-eye maple, approximately 6" high.
"Katschen" means "little cat" in German.
That was the name we gave our first cat.

GRAIN

Photocopy at 100%

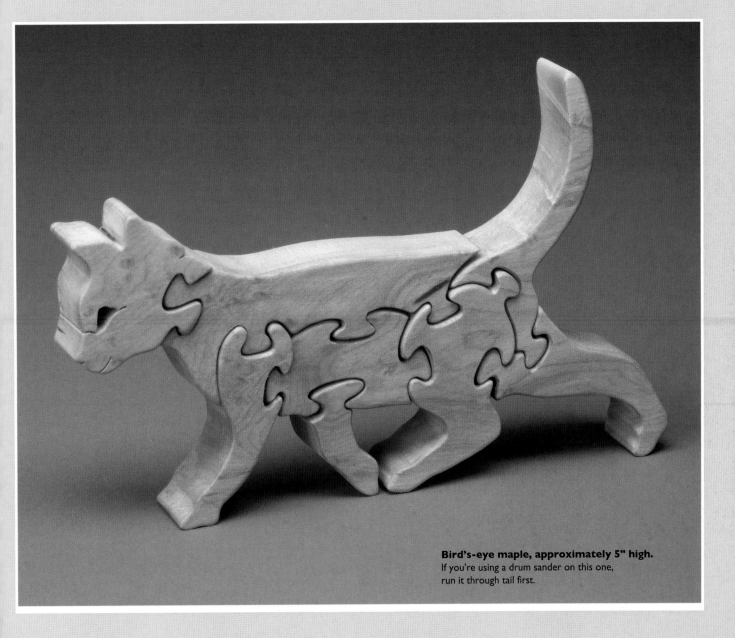

Bird's-eye maple, approximately 5" high.
If you're using a drum sander on this one,
run it through tail first.

GRAIN

Photocopy at 125%

Cats Being Cats

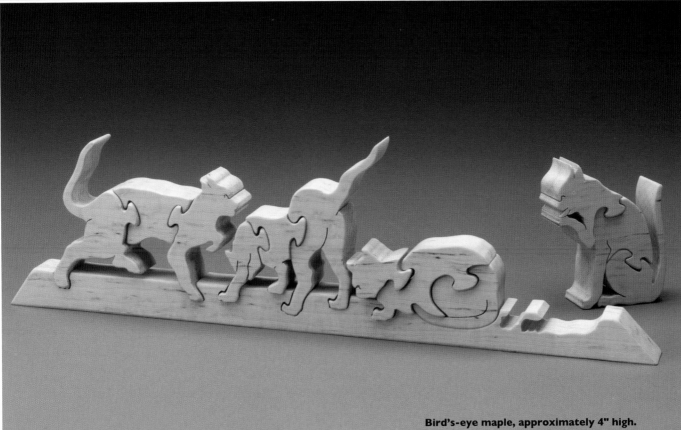

Bird's-eye maple, approximately 4" high.
A friend asked for four cats, just being cats. Note that this design is not drum-sander safe.

GRAIN

Photocopy at 100%

Gonçalo alves, approximately 4" high.
This is an Abyssinian Guinea Pig. It has the fanciest coat.

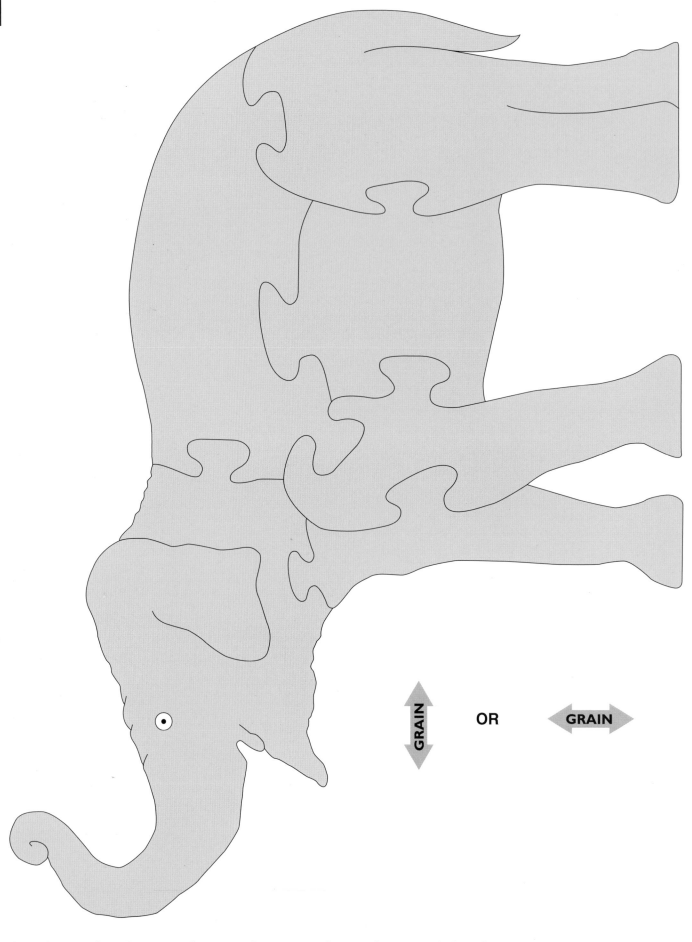

GRAIN OR GRAIN

Cherry, approximately 7" high.
This is an Indian elephant, as requested by a customer.

Photocopy at 105%

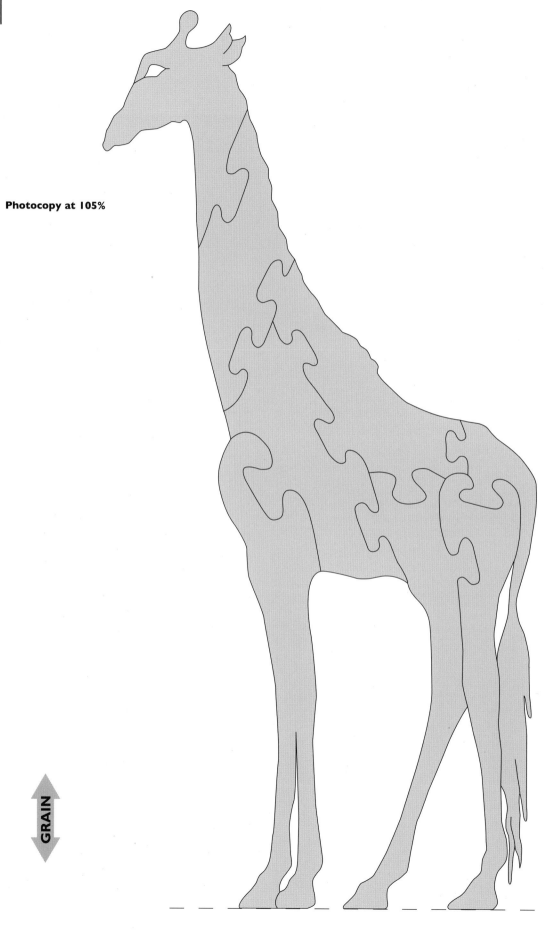

GRAIN

Australian lacewood, approximately 10" high.
Lacewood actually comes from Australia.
Its American cousin is the sycamore tree.
I always check the feet to be sure they're flat.
It stands much better.

GRAIN

Photocopy at 100%

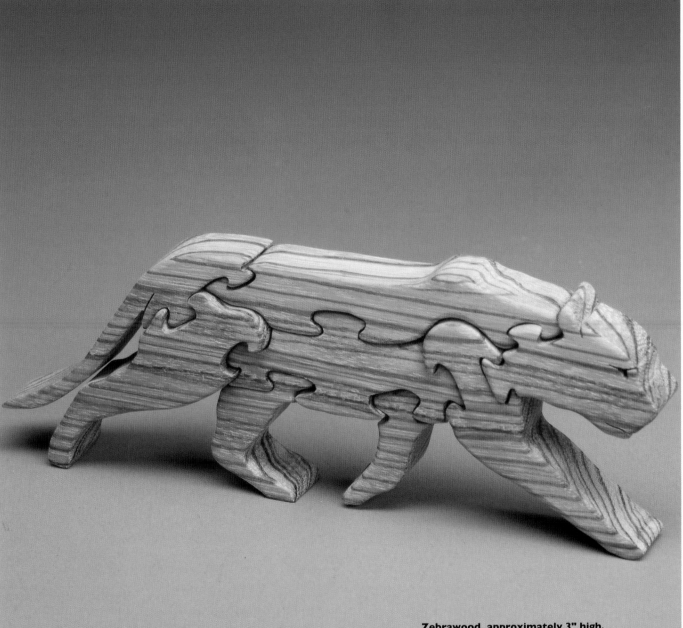

Zebrawood, approximately 3" high.
Zebrawood makes a pretty good tiger, even
if the stripes go the wrong way.

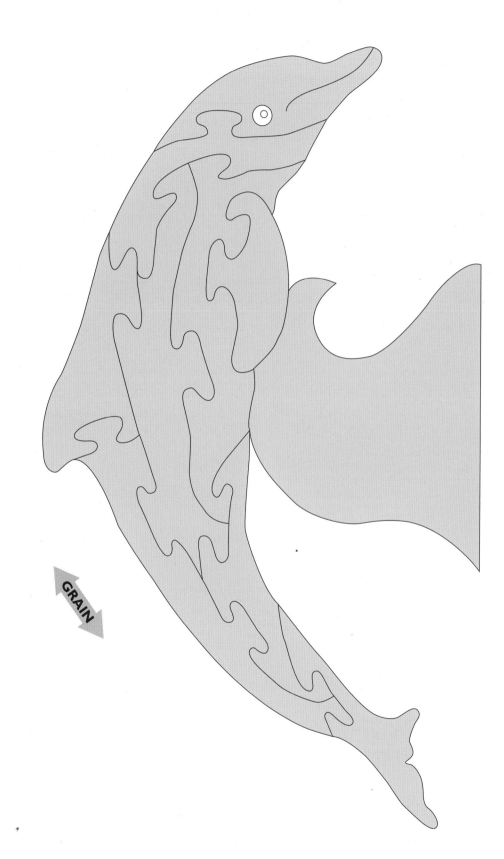

GRAIN

Photocopy at 100%

Walnut, approximately 5" high.
He really needed a wave. If you're using a
drum sander on this one, cut it with a frame
around it as shown in the tip box on page 15.

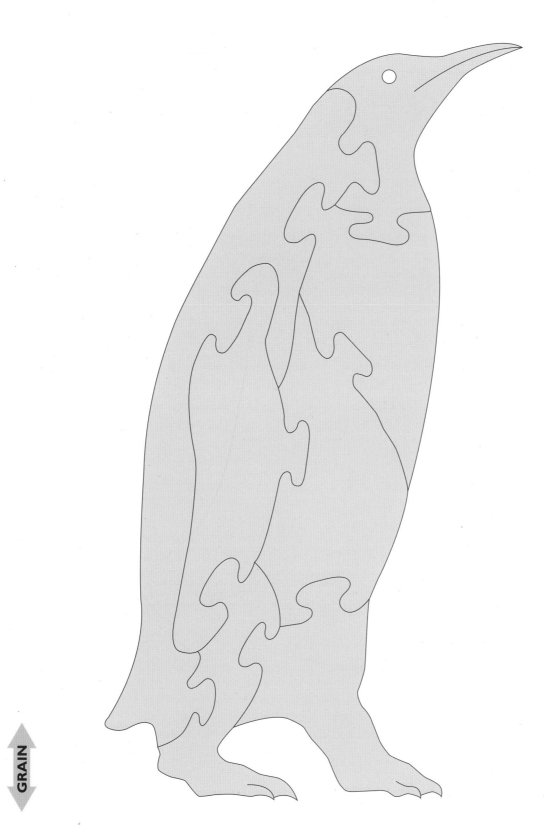

GRAIN

Photocopy at 100%

Aspen, approximately 8" high.
Our customers used to buy penguins when
they were a solid color, but when I went to
black and white, sales quadrupled! See the
instructions in the Finishing section on page
14 to dye the project.

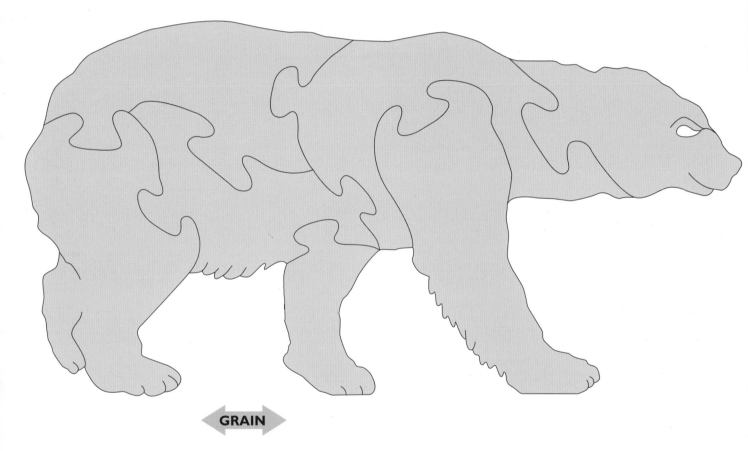

GRAIN

Photocopy at 100%

Aspen, approximately 4" high.
Polar Bears should be white.

GRAIN

Photocopy at 100%

Tree Frog

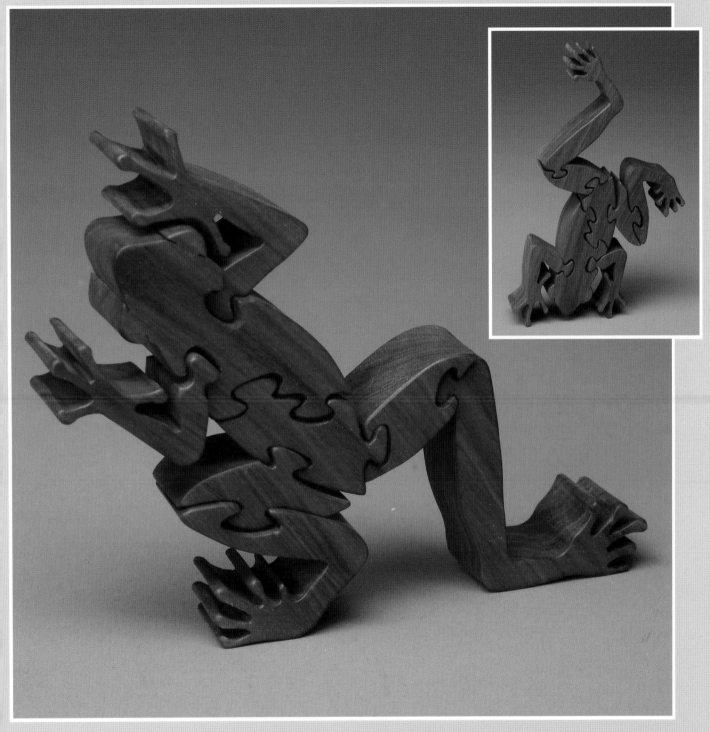

Chakte kok, approximately 7" high.
Red appears to be the wood color of choice for
tree frogs. He'll dive if you've cut him right.

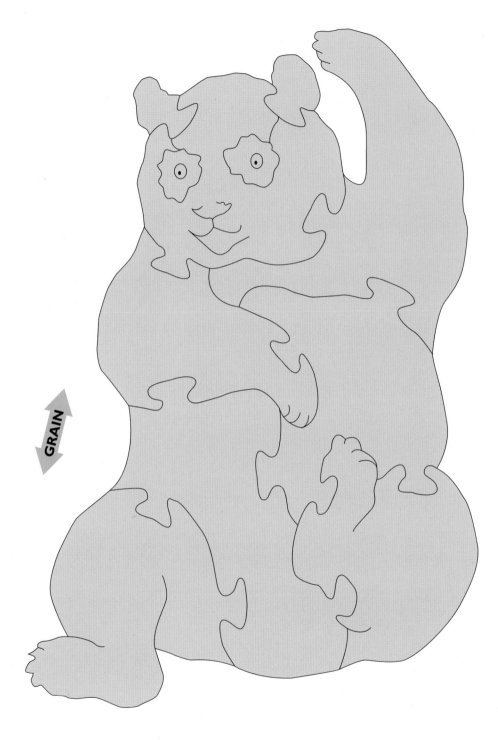

GRAIN

Photocopy at 100%

Aspen, approximately 7" high.
Another good idea from a customer. See the instructions in the
Finishing section on page 14 to dye the project.

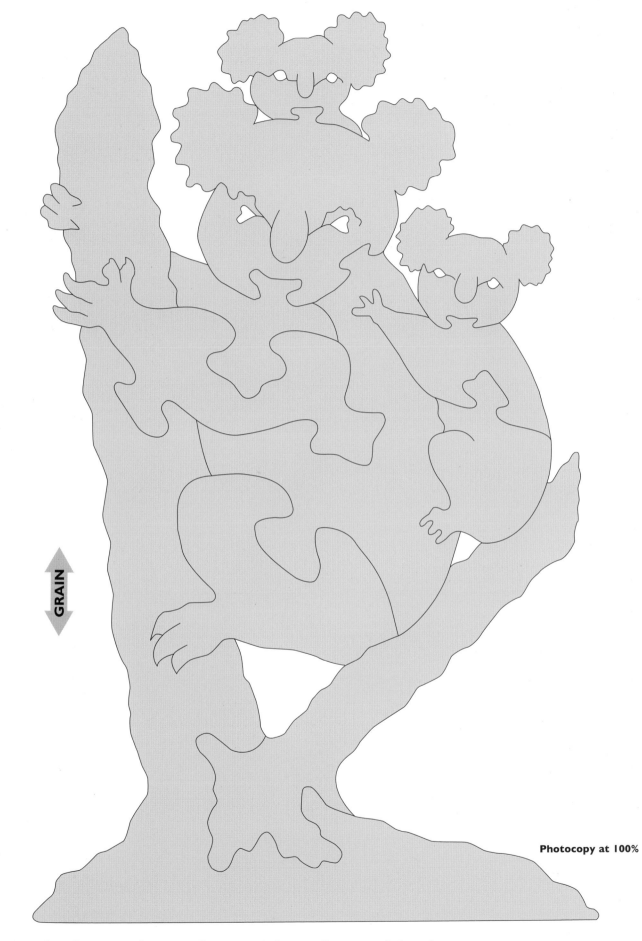

GRAIN

Photocopy at 100%

Ash, approximately 10" high.
This puzzle looks good in any wood.

I used Behlen's Jet Black stain on every other piece. As mentioned in the Finishing section on page 14, I let the dyed pieces dry overnight, assemble the puzzle (to make sure the correct pieces are together), and then oil all the pieces of the same cow at the same time.

Originally, I took two ¾" boards (one of aspen and one of Peruvian walnut), nailed them together, and stack-cut two at a time. I ended up with two "mirror-image" cows (one with a white head and one with a black head, etc.) and very sore elbows. It's hard work to push that much wood through a scroll saw! Dyeing every other piece is much more practical.

GRAIN

Photocopy at 100%

Holstein Cow

Aspen, approximately 5" high.
People like cows with black heads and
white udders or the "udder" way around.

GRAIN

Photocopy at 100%

Cherry, approximately 5" high.
This was specifically designed for a small child.
The pieces are sturdy.

GRAIN

Photocopy at 100%

Poplar, approximately 6" high.
This puzzle was modeled on a photo of this mare pulling a carriage. The mare's owner took the picture and gave me permission to use it. Frisians are always black! See the instructions in the Finishing section on page 14 to dye the project.

GRAIN

Photocopy at 100%

Cherry, approximately 4" high.
This photo shows the difference in color between the heartwood and the sapwood of cherry.

GRAIN

Photocopy at 100%

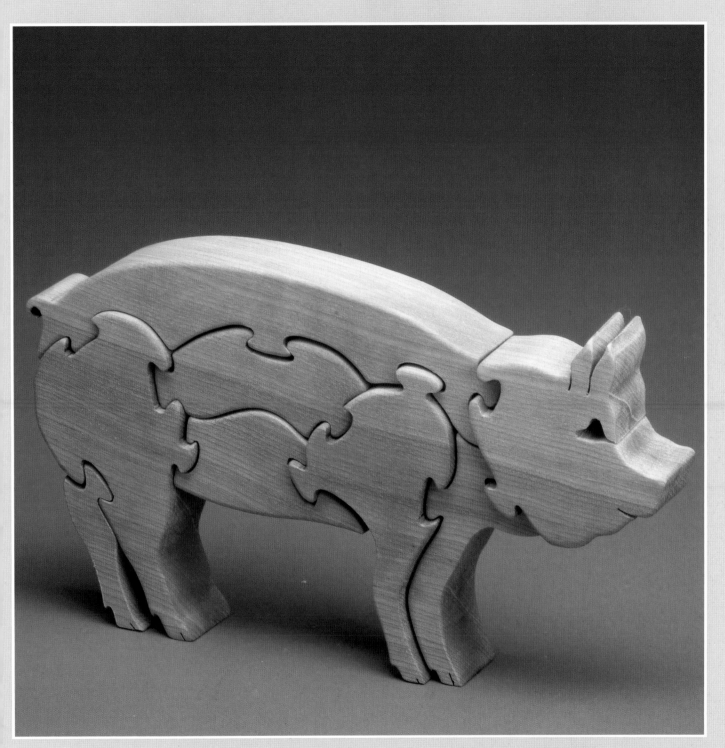

Birch, approximately 4" high.
The color change between the heartwood and
the sapwood of birch is much less pronounced.

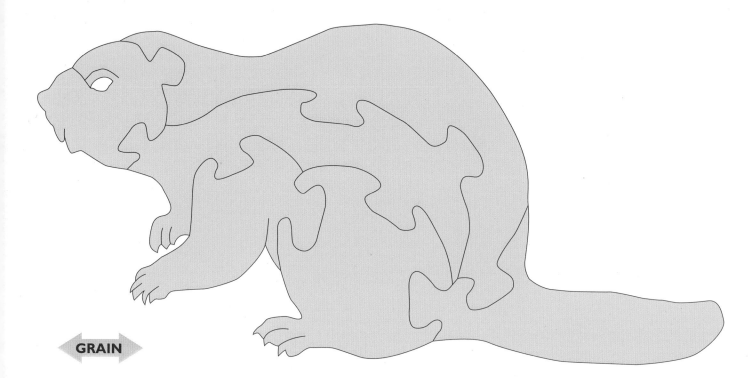

GRAIN

Photocopy at 100%

Walnut, approximately 4" high.
I never knew there were so many people named "Beaver"!

GRAIN

Photocopy at 100%

Mountain Lion

Birch, approximately 5" high.
I really like the angled face. The tail of the lion crunches in the drum sander, so don't use it!

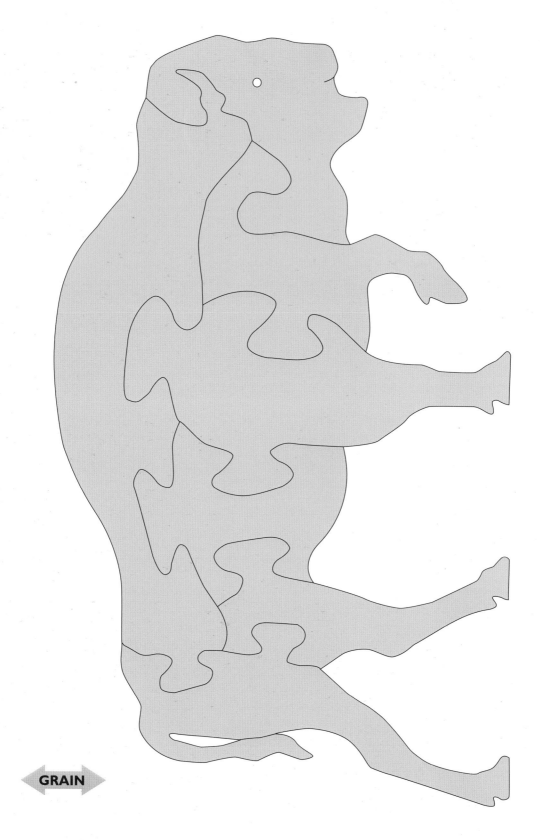

GRAIN

Photocopy at 100%

Bison

Walnut, approximately 5" high.
This design was an exercise in frustration. He's so front heavy that the first three I made fell on their noses (so keep trying with your own patterns).

GRAIN

Photocopy at 100%

Cherry, approximately 5" high.
I have fond memories of boards.
This was a particularly pretty one.

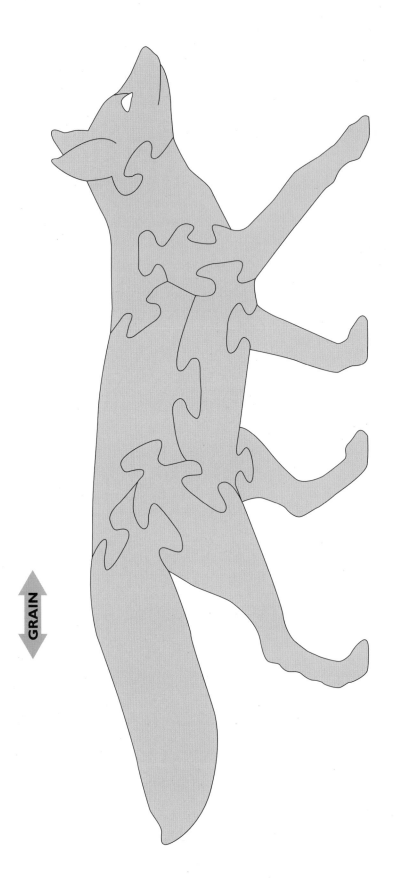

GRAIN

Photocopy at 100%

Padauk, approximately 3" high.
Padauk is the perfect wood for a red fox. Note that this design is not drum-sander safe.

GRAIN

Photocopy at 100%

Aspen, approximately 6" high.
All of the snow-country creatures are cut in aspen.

GRAIN

Photocopy at 100%

Walnut, approximately 7" high.
The color difference in the heartwood and
the sapwood of walnut is often striking.

GRAIN

Photocopy at 100%

Cherry, approximately 8" high.
A magnificent rack of antlers graces this caribou. Note that this design is not drum-sander safe.

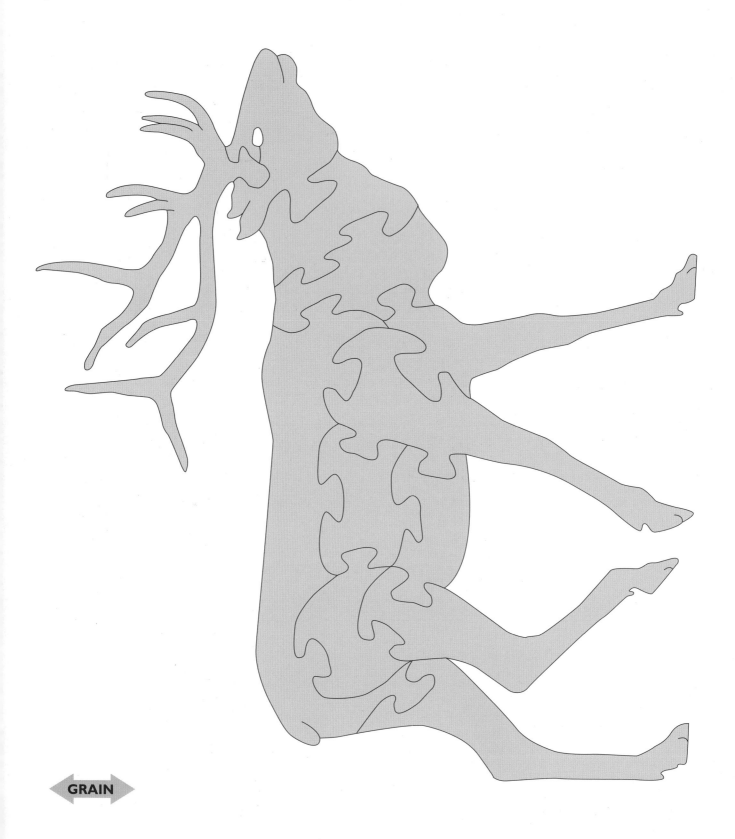

GRAIN

Photocopy at 100%

Walnut, approximately 7" high.
Another magnificent rack of antlers—sand very
cautiously. Note that this design is not drum-sander safe.

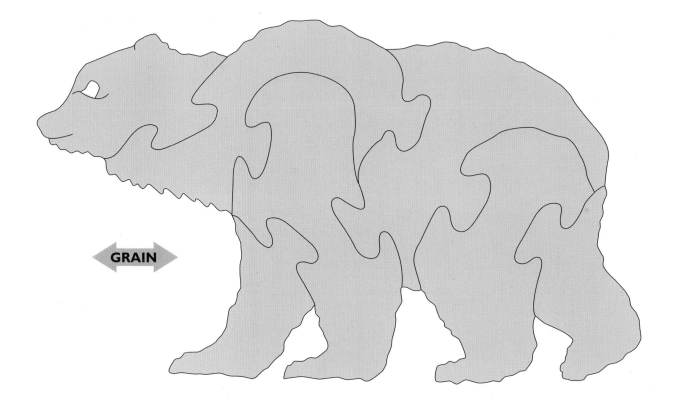

GRAIN

Photocopy at 100%

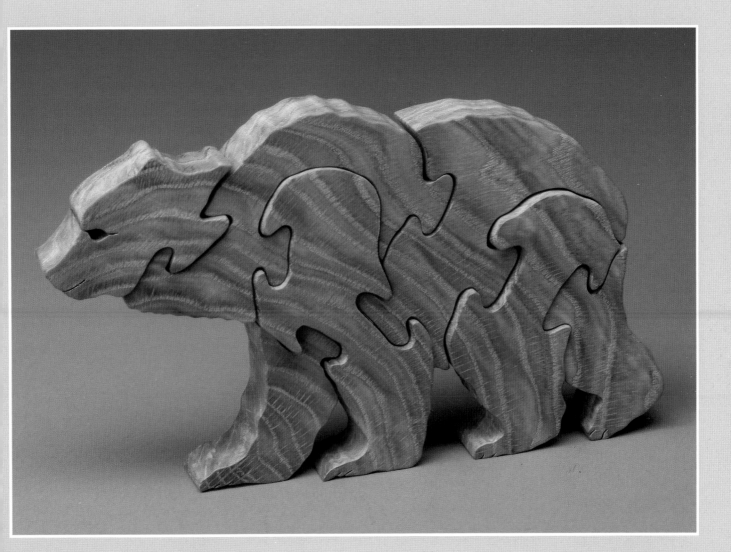

Oak, approximately 7" high.
Both the Brown Bear and the Squirrel
(page 110) were cut from the same board.
It had a swirl of wild grain at one end,
merging into straight grain farther down.
The board had a lot of color variation. This
was another board I remember fondly.

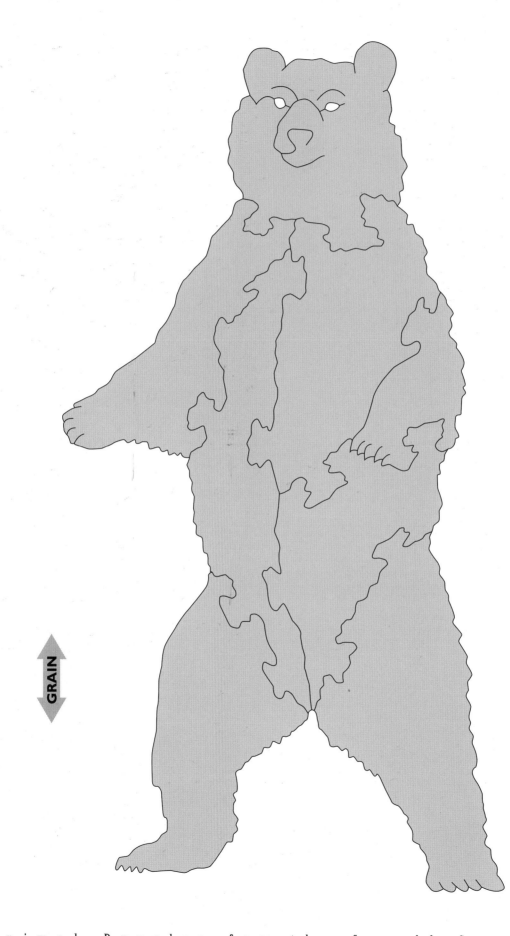

GRAIN

Photocopy at 100%

Grizzly Bear

Walnut, approximately 8" high.
This was done from a photo taken through
Plexiglas at a little nature museum.

GRAIN

Photocopy at 100%

Oak, approximately 5" high.
The Squirrel is holding an acorn, but,
for variety, you can use the hickory nut.

GRAIN

Photocopy at 100%

Imbuia, approximately 4" high.
This wood is sort of greenish. I use it for turtles, Green Men, and the occasional alligator. Note that this design is not drum-sander safe.

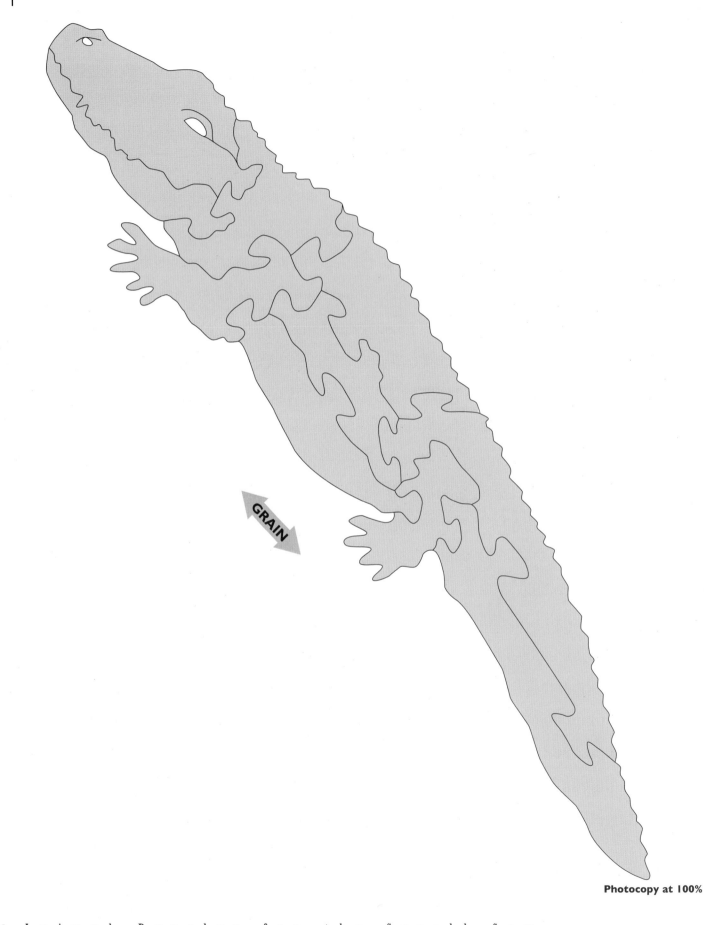

GRAIN

Photocopy at 100%

Walnut, approximately 2" high.
If you check, you'll find that the number of toes is accurate.

GRAIN

Photocopy at 115%

Gonçalo alves, approximately 10" high.
Yes, the fish is too big, but I needed a base. It's a Muskie. Note
that this design is not drum-sander safe.

Photocopy at 100%

Quail Family

Sycamore; one chick in cherry. Approximate heights: Papa—7", Mama—5", Babies—2".
We were in Arizona and saw families of quail everywhere. There is always a sentinel on guard with other quail scurrying around feeding, and at the right time of year, a lot of chicks.

Note that this design is not drum-sander safe.

Photocopy at 100%

Photocopy at 150%

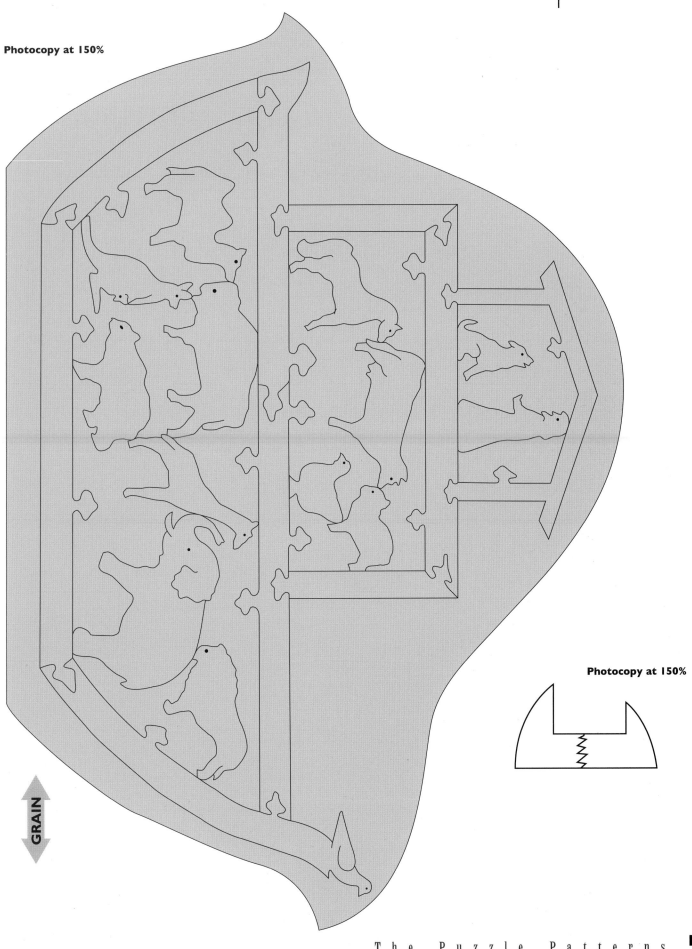

GRAIN

Photocopy at 150%

Noah's Ark

Cherry, approximately 9" high (Ark alone).
With the frame in place, you can run this puzzle through the drum sander.

I cut a backer board from ¼" Baltic birch for this landscape puzzle. It's cut a little larger than the finished puzzle. Without the backer board, this puzzle is impossible to pick up or lay down without having pieces fall out. This puzzle can be displayed freestanding or (if you use the stands) with the backer board in place.

Cut the stands from the same board from which the puzzle is cut. You'll need two stands. Adjust the width of the stands to fit your puzzle thickness, plus the thickness of the backer board. The stand pattern is included on page 74.

Each creature must be sliced in half to create the "two by two" that goes with the ark. (See the instructions for turning one baby rabbit into three on pages 10 and 11.)

See page 26 for instructions on drilling the eyes. If you have a drum sander, cut a frame around the outside of the ark. You can then use the frame as a carrier to avoid breakage in the drum sander. See page 15 for more information on carriers.

With landscape puzzles that I expect children to play with, I oil all of the pieces. Bare wood picks up fingerprints because it does not have the oil to protect it.

I finished this puzzle with Behlen's Cherry stain on the positive pieces. After the stained pieces were dry, I dipped them in Danish Oil Natural. I also dipped the background pieces in Danish Oil Natural.

Index

More Great Project Books from Fox Chapel Publishing

Fantasy & Legend Scroll Saw Puzzles
By Judy & Dave Peterson

25 easy-to-follow instructions for puzzles depicting fabled creatures from Greek mythology and other storied traditions.

ISBN: 978-1-56523-256-3
$14.95 • 80 Pages

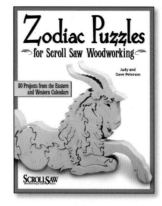

Zodiac Puzzles for Scroll Saw Woodworking
30 Projects from the Eastern and Western Calendars
By Judy and Dave Peterson

Crafters will find inspiration in the stars with this collection of scroll saw patterns based on the astrological signs of the Western and Chinese zodiacs.

ISBN 978-1-56523-393-5
$17.95 • 96 Pages

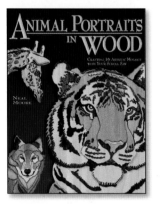

Animal Portraits in Wood
By Neal Moore

16 precisely designed and color-coded patterns for creating stunning segmented portraiture on your scroll saw.

ISBN: 978-1-56523-293-8
$17.95 • 128 Pages

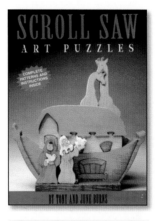

Scroll Saw Art Puzzles
By Tony & June Burns

32 enjoyable projects with all the step-by-step cutting and painting instructions you need.

ISBN: 978-1-56523-116-0
$ 14.95 • 88 Pages

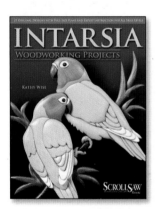

Intarsia Woodworking Projects
By Kathy Wise

From a celebrated intarsia artist comes 21 original full-size patterns. Included are step-by-step tutorials.

ISBN: 978-1-56523-339-3
$19.95 • 80 Pages

Wildlife Portraits in Wood
By Charles Dearing

Captures beautiful & fascinating wildlife scenery from around the world. Includes 30 attractive patterns to adorn your home.

ISBN: 978-1-56523-338-6
$14.95 • 72 Pages

WOODCARVING
ILLUSTRATED

In addition to being a leading source of woodworking books and DVDs, Fox Chapel also publishes Woodcarving Illustrated. Released quarterly, it delivers premium projects, expert tips and techniques from today's finest carvers, and in-depth information about the latest tools, equipment & materials.

Subscribe Today!
Woodcarving Illustrated: **888-506-6630**
www.FoxChapelPublishing.com

Look for These Books at Your Local Bookstore or Woodworking Retailer
To order direct, call **800-457-9112** or visit *www.FoxChapelPublishing.com*
By mail, please send check or money order + S&H to:
Fox Chapel Publishing, 1970 Broad Street, East Petersburg, PA 17520

# Item	US Shipping Rate
1 Item	$3.99
Each Additional	.99

Canadian & International Orders – please email info@foxchapelpublishing.com or visit our website for actual shipping costs.